Fans Love Reading
Choose Your Own Adventure®!

"My friends and I love to read these books. They all have exciting adventures and it feels like I am really there."

Nakaya Samuel, age 10

"The demand for these books never really abated and you have made this children's librarian's dream come true."

Marge Loch-Wouters,
Menasha Public Library, Menasha WI

"When I get to the end of the page, I want to keep going to find out what is going to happen to me. I get to make my own choices of what I WANT to happen next."

Bionca Samuel, age 10

Watch for these titles coming up in the

CHOOSE YOUR OWN ADVENTURE®

Dragonlark™ imprint

YOUR VERY OWN ROBOT
by R. A. Montgomery

INDIAN TRAIL
by R. A. Montgomery

CARAVAN
by R. A. Montgomery

THE HAUNTED HOUSE
by R. A. Montgomery

YOUR PURRR-FECT BIRTHDAY
by R. A. Montgomery

COMING IN SPRING 2008

THE FAIRY PRINCESS KIDNAP
by Shannon Gilligan

HAUNTED HARBOR
by Shannon Gilligan

MORE TITLES COMING SOON!

Ask your bookseller for books you have missed
or visit us at cyoa.com to learn more.

www.cyoa.com

CHOOSE YOUR OWN ADVENTURE®

BY R.A. MONTGOMERY

A DRAGONLARK BOOK

Illustrated by: Keith Newton
Book design: Stacey Boyd, Big Eyedea Visual Design

For information regarding permission, write to:

CHOOSECO
P.O. Box 46
Waitsfield, Vermont 05673
www.cyoa.com

A DRAGONLARK BOOK

ISBN: 1-933390-55-7
EAN: 978-1-933390-55-0

Published simultaneously in the United States and Canada

Printed in the United States

0 9 8 7 6 5 4 3 2 1

To S, who taught me to love birthdays....

A DRAGONLARK BOOK

READ THIS FIRST!!!

WATCH OUT!
THIS BOOK IS DIFFERENT
than *every* book you've ever read.

Don't believe me?

Have you *ever* read a book that was about YOU?

This book is!

YOU get to choose what happens next
—and even how the story will end.

DON'T READ THIS BOOK FROM
THE FIRST PAGE TO THE LAST.

Read until you reach a choice.
Turn to the page of the choice you like best.
If you don't like the end you reach, just start over!

Tomorrow is your birthday. You can hardly wait. There is just one problem.

For the last eleven days your cat Festus has done some very strange things. First he left a dead mouse next to your backpack. Then he made you a gift of some broken cat toys while you were at school. Finally, he put two dirty socks on your pillow.

In the past two days, Festus has left you notes paw-scratched on toilet paper. The markings are strange. Is it in cat language?

You decide to ask your parents.

Turn to page 3.

"Hey mom. Do you think this says anything?" you ask holding up the shredded toilet paper.

Your mother looks down. "Where did you get that? It looks like hieroglyphics."

"What are hieroglyphics?" you ask.

"One of the first writing systems invented. From ancient Egypt," your mother explains. "Why are you writing hieroglyphs on toilet paper?" she asks.

"It's not me. Festus did it," you reply.

You mother just laughs. "Well, cats did used to be royal kings in ancient Egypt."

You look down at Festus. He's washing his ears. He looks up.

"What does it say, Fes?" you ask.

Fes just meows and continues to clean.

If you decide to look up a hieroglyph alphabet to see if Festus really is sending a message, turn to page 48.

If you decide you would rather to go to bed so that your birthday gets here sooner, turn to page 5.

You decide to go to bed so your birthday will come sooner. You dream you are on a camping trip. Your sleeping bag is too tight. When you wake up, you try to throw back the covers. But you can't move! You look around. You are trapped under your blanket. Fes has tucked it in tight all the way around! There is no way out.

"Festus!" you yell. "Fes, what are you doing? Let me out."

"I am right here," he replies. "No need to shout."

That's strange. Festus is speaking English. Is this still part of your dream? You pinch yourself to make sure.

Turn to page 6.

"First, make a birthday wish," Festus commands.

"My wish is to get out of here. It's hot under the blanket," you shout. Festus chuckles. "Patience is a virtue," he adds in his know-it-all voice. Sometimes you just hate Festus.

"So, my dear human, you have a choice. Would you like to spend your birthday in the world of ancient Egypt? Think pyramids, sand, deserts, the Nile River. It was a time when cats ruled all of Egypt and the rest of the world!"

"Right now," you tell Fes, "a world ruled by cats does not seem like a great idea."

"Well, then," Festus answers, "your other choice is the World of Birthdays Never Imagined. It's risky but lots of fun."

It is clear Festus will do nothing until you make a choice.

If you decide to travel to Ancient Egypt, turn to page 9.

If you decide to travel to the World of Birthdays Never Imagined, turn to page 34.

10:05PM

"OK," you agree. "Ancient Egypt as long as we're back in time for my birthday party."

"Very good choice," Festus says as he pulls the sheets and blanket back.

"What do I do now?" you ask.

"Take this hairball and make some tea out of it," Festus orders. He is purring again. This is always a danger sign.

"Tea out of a hairball. Festus, are you crazy?!!!!" you cry.

But you do it. The tea is grey and slimy. It smells like fog and burning garbage.

"One, two, three and down it goes," Fes orders in his best cat-wheedling voice.

Turn to page 10.

You take a sip of hairball tea and gag.

"Finish it," Fes says. This time he is speaking in Egyptian.

As you drink the last bits, your skin begins to tingle. The room begins to spin.

Zoceroo!! Suddenly, you are outside. It is night. The moon is high overhead. You and Festus are standing next to a wide river. Palm trees line the banks. And sand stretches in every direction. Are those pyramids sticking up in the distance?

"Wow. Festus. We're in Egypt."

"Ancient Egypt," Festus says. "And here I am King."

Turn to page 12.

You look down. Fes is still a cat. But he is wearing a crown shaped like a strange motorcycle helmet. It is covered in jewels. He carries a scepter with a snake's head on top.

"Today is my birthday. It is also your birthday. We are related," Fes announces in a kingly new voice.

"I was afraid of that," you say.

"Celebrations for our birthdays begin at dawn. The Sun Boat tied to that dock just below can take us there," Festus announces grandly. "Let's climb aboard."

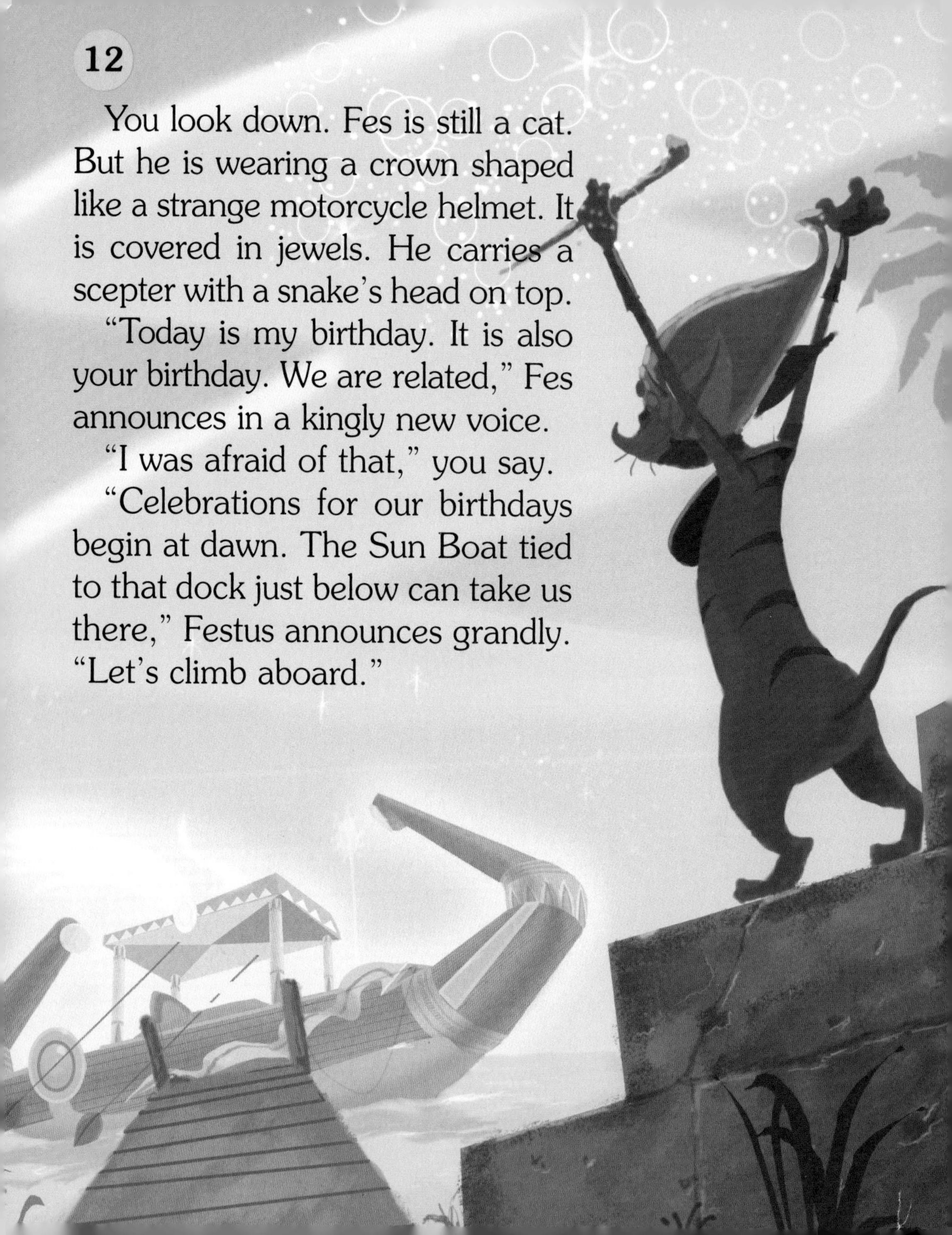

For the first time you notice your pajamas are gone and you are wearing sandals and a short linen tunic. You follow Festus to the dock. Two tall guards stand to either side. One of them shouts, "Halt!"

Turn to page 15.

"Where did you get that scepter?" the guard demands.

"It is mine," Festus says in his best kingly voice.

"It looks like the scepter stolen from the Pharaoh's palace," the other guard says.

You glance at Festus. Up until now, you have both been speaking Egyptian. But he suddenly says in human English, "Time to get out of here."

There are exactly two choices. You can make a dash for the boat. Or you can head into the sand dunes toward the pyramids.

If you decide to dash for the boat, turn to page 22.

If you decide to head for the sand dunes, turn to page 16.

You decide to run for the dunes. You point in that direction with your big toe. Festus nods. Without another word, you make a run for it.

You run as fast as you can without looking back. You run past a small village filled with mud houses. You run past a field of grain and an orchard of date palms. You can hear the guards shouting behind you. Time to hide! You spy a small shack on the edge of the field. Your other choice is the desert straight ahead.

If you decide to stop and hide in the shack, turn to page 20.

If you decide to keep running straight into the sand dunes, turn to page 17.

There is a tall sand dune straight ahead. You and Festus huff and puff your way to the top.

When you can see over the edge, you stop and gasp. On the other side is a beautiful valley filled with pyramids. You stop to catch your breath.

"It's the Valley of the Kings," Festus says. "With some of the greatest pyramids in Egypt."

You hear someone shouting from behind. The guards!

"Better get going," Festus says. "Follow me."

You run toward the pyramids.

"What now Fes?" you cry.

"Run into the funeral chamber of the first pyramid," he answers. "They'll never come in."

"Why?" you cry.

"Because when you go in you may never come out!" Festus shouts.

Turn to page 18.

"Never come out?" you cry.

"You have a better idea?" Festus replies. The two guards are less than 100 yards away. It looks like you don't have a choice.

You follow Festus into the pyramid. It's pitch black inside and very quiet. The guards do not follow.

"Wow, I'm tired," you say. "Think it's okay to take a nap?"

But Festus doesn't answer. He's already snoring.

When you wake up, you are back home in in your bedroom. But things are different. You notice there are bars on your bed.

Festus sits nearby, licking his paws. His Egyptian crown is gone. He looks like a regular cat again.

"Festus, what is going on?" you ask.

But instead of words, your voice comes out gurgles.

The door opens. It's your dad.

"Dad! It's me!" you cry. Again, it comes out sounding like baby talk.

Your dad reaches over the bars. He looks really big. He scoops you up in his arms. Then it hits you: you're back home alright. But something is wrong. When you fell asleep in the pyramid, you went back in time. You're a baby again!

"Hey there! Happy birthday!" your dad says giving you a big kiss on your forehead. He lifts you out of the crib. "One year old today!" he says with a smile.

You look at Festus who smiles sweetly.

He's going to pay for this!

The End

"Festus," you say, pointing. "The shack!"

"Right," Festus answers. You duck inside just in time. The two guards run past.

Your eyes get used to the dark, and you see something shiny on the ground.

"Look Festus. A lamp," you say, holding a small brass lamp up to the moonlight that comes in the window.

"Watch out," Festus warns.

"What do you mean?" you ask.

"Don't rub it," Festus answers.

"Like you think it's magic? If I rub it and make a wish?" You start to laugh. "Festus, you old worrier, I'm not afraid!"

You rub the lamp. Festus squeezes his eyes shut.

"See? Nothing happens," you say.

Just then you hear a breeze rustle in the trees.

"You'll be sorry," Festus says.

Another gust of wind blows. And another.

Soon the wind in the trees is starting to whistle.

You step outside. A fine mist of sand is filling the air.

"A sandstorm!" you yell, coughing.

"I told you not to rub the lamp," Festus says. "And it's called a *Simoon*, not a sand storm."

The wind grows louder and stronger. You both huddle inside. You squeeze your eyes and mouth shut but the sand is coming in your nose! Yuck!

"Fes! We're doomed!" you shout. You can barely hear your voice over the howl of the wind.

Turn to page 41.

You motion toward the boat. And run for it. The guards dive after you. But they trip into each other. Festus leaps into the boat first. You push away from the small landing just in time. The guards stand on the dock, shouting and waving their arms.

"I thought you said you were King," you sputter, guiding the tiller through the rapid current.

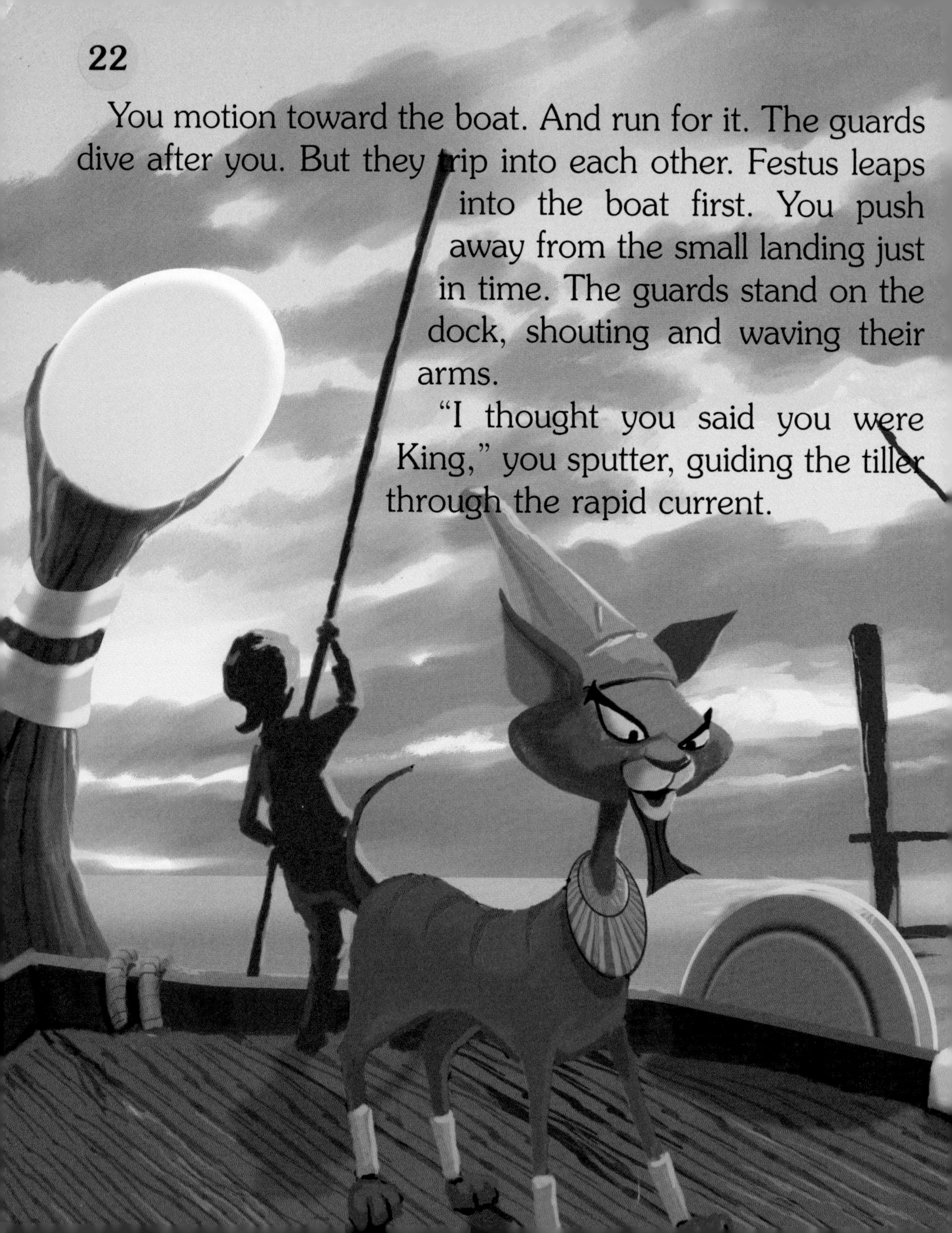

"I am," Festus replies. He has that guilty look. "But there are nine of us."

"Great. I'm in ancient Egypt for less than five minutes and I'm already in trouble. What now, oh Great One?" you ask.

Festus scans the horizon. "I have one hairball left. We can make some more hairball tea and go home. Or we can head to the ancient city of Memphis. Memphis is the capital of Egypt. That's where we can return the scepter to the palace."

If you decide to make another cup of hairball tea, turn to page 24.

If you decide to return the scepter to Memphis,turn to page 29.

"I vote for hairball tea," you reply. "I'm beginning to like it."

Festus laughs at your joke. You pull the boat over at the next village. Fes buys a cup of boiled water from a shop-keeper. No one gives you a second look. It was a good idea to leave the scepter and crown in the boat, you think.

You make the hairball tea. It doesn't work this time. You drink the whole cup but nothing happens.

Turn to page 26.

You carefully unwrap the present.

"Go on," Festus urges. "It won't bite. I promise."

You tug one of the gold ribbons. Then you pull another ribbon.

Inside the box is a cage. Inside the cage is a golden python!!!! The python smiles at you with the sweetest snake smile you have ever seen.

"Festus! How did you know? I've always wanted a golden python!" you say.

"I just knew, old pal. Cats know all. Happy birthday!" he replies.

What a great and magical birthday it is, you think.

The End

You hear a yell from the river's shore. Someone has found the scepter and crown! A small mob of people are running toward you, pointing and shouting, "It's them!"

"Uh-oh. What now?" Festus asks.

"Run for it!" you yell.

You duck into a narrow alley. Festus is right behind.

It sounds like half the town is running after you. You turn around to take a look. They are!

Turn to page 28.

Festus runs ahead and you follow. He takes a left, then a right. The streets get narrower.

You follow Festus around a corner. It's a dead end! You're facing a tall stone wall. What now?

You look back. "They're getting closer!" you cry.

"They're also getting fuzzier and fuzzier," Festus comments.

He's right. Everyone is a little blurry around the edges. What's happening?

ZOCEROO!

Turn to page 42.

"I say we return the scepter to Memphis," you tell Festus.

"Good choice. That's where they will be holding our birthday party," he answers.

The two of you travel along the Nile through the night. Stars gleam in the sky. You drift past villages and farms. clustered next to the riverbanks. The farmers need to capture the rich silt the spring floods deposit on their fields every year.

At dawn, the city of Memphis comes into view. By the time you reach the port, it is bustling with traders and boatmen. You are busy rowing, trying not to hit any other boats. You glance up to see Festus, posed in the bow of the boat, holding the scepter.

Everybody is bowing down to him!

"This is going to go straight to your head," you say to Festus. But he is waving to his subjects. He's not listening.

Turn to page 30.

An important-looking man steps forward as you tie up to the dock. He bows deeply.

"Your highness, we have been waiting for your arrival to begin," he announces.

"Begin what?" you ask.

"The birthday festivities, of course," he replies. "Everyone at the palace is waiting. Who are you?"

"That's my new servant," Festus answers jauntily.

You glower at Festus. *"Servant?"* you ask.

He just smiles.

"To the palace," Festus commands. He points with his scepter like a king.

Turn to page 32.

The palace is near the port. Everyone in the streets who sees Festus bows low and yells, "Happy Birthday, your highness!"

At the palace the other eight princes greet Festus warmly. Two of the other princes are also cats. Each prince sits on a throne in front of a large pile of presents. As soon as Festus sits in the last empty throne, everyone starts unwrapping.

"Here," Festus says, handing you a box wrapped in beautiful gold fabric. "This one is yours. I want to share."

"Why thanks Fes, old cat," you say. You are touched by his generosity. After all, it is your birthday too.

You reach to accept the box. It emits a low, nasty hissing sound.

Festus smiles and licks his paw.

The hissing gets louder.

Turn to page 25.

"How do we get you the world of Birthdays Never Imagined?" you ask. "Easy," Festus replies. "Follow me."

Fes jumps up and pulls open the latch of your bedroom door.

You follow Festus as he trots up the hallway. He enters the bathroom. Then he continues through to the linen closet.

"Here."

He points to a door at the back of the closet.

"I've never seen that door before," you tell your cat.

"That's because you've never looked," Festus replies airily.

Before you can turn the handle, the door slowly swings forward.

Turn to the next page.

The closet door opens into a huge room. The ceilings are so far away, you can't see them. Right in front of you, there is a strange machine. It looks like a giant salad spinner with lights.

"What's that?" you ask.

"It's a time-space machine," Festus answers. "With a spin, you hurtle through space and time. Best of all, we can stop wherever you like. Just press the red lighted button."

Together you hop in. Once you are inside, the spinning starts. At first it is slow. Then you go faster and faster. You notice words flashing on a screen near the red button.

FRENCH REVOLUTION. INDIA. HENRY FORD. ELEANOR ROOSEVELT. KING HENRY V. BELTED GALLOWAYS. MATA HARI. THE WHEEL. THOMAS EDISON. DAKOTA SIOUX. GHENGHIS KHAN. HO CHI MINH. THE RING CYCLE. KEYSTONE ARCH. HAGIA SOPHIA. PALAZZO PISANI....

If you decide to press the red button now,
turn to page 38.

If you decide to wait a little longer to press the button, *turn to page 51.*

If you say, "Festus, you press the button",
turn to page 44.

You reach toward the red button and press. It is hot to the touch when you press.

SCREECH!!!! The time-space machine makes a loud metal sound as it slows down. The screen says:

THE BEGINNING OF TIME

"Holy mackerel," you say. You get out of the salad spinner. You stand in the great, empty void of space without limits. There is no light. No sound. No wind. No heat. No nothing.

"Where are we, Fes?" you squeak.

"We are at the beginning of time," he replies in a hushed voice. "Just hold your horses."

Turn to page 40.

"What do you mean, the beginning of time?" you ask.

"Like I said. the very real beginning of time, the start of the universe. Shhhh..." Fes says.

"But, Fes, we're here. Now. How can................"

You hear a hiss. It is getting louder and louder. Soon it is the loudest sound you have ever heard.

Zaaaaoshhhhhhhhh!! Zarrrooooooooom!!

Brilliant light, brighter than all the stars in the universe.

Expansion.

Waves.

Pulses.

The birth of the universe takes place before your very own eyes.

This is the great singularity—that moment/non-moment in time-space when all that we know came into existence.

The big bang without sound.

The great expansion without limit.

The unknowable.

The birthday of the universe!!!!!!!!!!

Happy birthday to everyone in the future, including you!!!!

The Beginning
and
The End

"Not yet, we're not," Festus shouts.

"Eat this magic sock," Festus commands. "You get half and I get half."

You don't argue. Down it goes. Yuckeroo.

ZAMAROOCHEEE!

You and Festus are back home, safe in your bed. It's morning. Your mom has the vacuum going in the dining room, getting ready for your party.

Was it all a dream? You look around. Festus stares you right in the eye. He looks like he is covered in a slight coat of dust.

"How's that for a purr-fect birthday surprise?" he wants to know.

"Hahaha, Fes," you say.

The End

"Honey, wake up. It's me," you mom says.

"What?" you ask, sitting up. You look around. You are in bed. It's dark outside.

"What time is it?" you ask.

"The middle of the night. It was just a bad dream," your mom whispers. She checks your forehead to make sure you don't have a fever.

You look down at the foot of your bed. Festus is cleaning his ears.

"Festus and I were back in ancient Egypt. A mob was chasing us. It was so real," you say.

"Some dreams can be that way. Now back to sleep."

Your mom gives you a kiss and turns out the light.

"Festus, was that a dream or was that real?" you demand as soon as your mom shuts the door.

Festus yawns a regal cat yawn. Then he smiles and gives you a wink. "Hairball tea works every time."

The End

"Festus, you press the button," you say.

"Fine with me!" he replies. He reaches out a paw, and... ZAP!!

You are standing in a tall room filled rows of desks.

Several men* are seated at the desks, arranged in half circles. Most of them are wearing headphones. There is a row of flags around the back of the room. You have never seen so many different flags.

The man at a large table in front of the room stands to announce, "The voting shall begin."

One by one each person stands and speaks into a microphone.

Turn to page 46.

*If it were up to you and Festus, an equal number of women would have been seated at this table.

"Argentina votes yes."

"Belgium votes yes."

"Brazil votes yes."

"Votes yes for what?" you wonder.

"Votes yes for the United Nations charter," Festus replies. "It's October 24th, 1945. If my history is correct, we are in the San Francisco Opera House. This is the birth of the United Nations.

"Canada votes yes."

"Chile votes yes."

"The United Nations has a birthday?" you ask.

"Everyone and everything has a birthday," Festus replies. "There isn't a day that goes by where it isn't someone's birthday someplace. Pretty great, huh? Every single day is a birthday."

"You're right, Festus. Pretty great," you reply, rubbing his ears in the special spot.

The End

"They're signing the Declaration. The Declaration of Independence! We're separating from England," the newsboy cries.

Someone rushes up to buy a paper.

It's the birth of the United States. Thirteen American colonies declare freedom from the King.

It's the birth of a nation.

It's the birth of freedom for all.

All people are considered equal.

What a birthday! And you are there!!!!!

The End

You decide to look up a hieroglyph alphabet.

Here is what the message says (or at least you think this is what it says):

You are a little embarrassed, but you are afraid of the old barn. You are getting too old to be afraid of the dark. "There's nothing to be afraid of," you say to yourself out loud.

You step out the back door. The barn is right there, big, black and empty. You start to whistle. Festus trots along right beside you. If something bad happens, Fes would get your parents. You slow down as you get closer. You take one step into the empty blackness.

Turn to the next page.

This is not so bad, you think. You continue until you are at the top of the ladder. Then you hear it. Someone is in the barn! You are sure!

You turn to try to climb back down. Thwomp! Everything goes black.

When you wake up, you are staring up at your parents. Sam, is there too. And your aunt and uncle and…

"Mom, what happened?" you ask.

"Sweetheart, it was supposed to be a surprise. An early birthday party. But you ran and tripped before we could turn on the lights," your Mom replies.

"Are you okay?" your Dad asks.

You look around. All your friends are there too. The barn is decorated with streamers and lights. Wow. It really was a party.

"I have just one question," you reply. "Is there any cake left?"

Everyone laughs.

The End

You wait a few more seconds. More words flash by on the small screen. The time-space machine continues to spin.

MOHENJO-DARO DALAI LAMA AMAZON RIVER INCA GOLD AVIGNON POPES CLEOPATRA D.W. GRIFFITH

"This better be good, Fes," you say as you press the button.

Turn to page 53.

CUCKOO BUSH

There is a flash of bright light and a puff of smoke. You look around. Festus is right beside you. The two of you are standing on a busy city street filled with horses and carriages. People are running in an out of a building across the street.

"Where are we?" you ask out loud.

A young boy selling papers overhears you,

"You're in Philadelphia, Pennsylvania! In the Americas! It's July 4th, 1776. History is being made!"

History? What history? you think.

Turn to page 47.

ABOUT THE AUTHOR

At the Temple of Literature and National University (Van Mieu-Quoc Tu Giam) in Hanoi, Vietnam

R. A. MONTGOMERY has hiked in the Himalayas, climbed mountains in Europe, scuba-dived in Central America, and worked in Africa. He lives in France in the winter, travels frequently to Asia, and calls Vermont home. Montgomery graduated from Williams College and attended graduate school at Yale University and NYU. His interests include macro-economics, geo-politics, mythology, history, mystery novels, and music. He has two grown sons, a daughter-in-law, and two granddaughters. His wife, Shannon Gilligan, is an author and noted interactive game designer. Montgomery feels that the new generation of people under 15 is the most important asset in our world.

For games, activities and other fun stuff, or to write to R. A. Montgomery, visit us online at CYOA.com

CREDITS

Illustrator: Keith Newton began his art career in the theater as a set painter. Having talent and a strong desire to paint portraits, he moved to New York and studied fine art at the Art Students League. Keith has won numerous awards in art such as The Grumbacher Gold Medallion and Salmagundi Award for Pastel. He soon began illustrating and was hired by Disney Feature Animation where he worked on such films as *Pocahontas* and *Mulan* as a background artist. Keith also designed color models for sculptures at Disney Animal Kingdom and has animated commercials for Euro Disney. Today, Keith Newton freelances from his home and teaches entertainment illustration at The College for Creative Studies in Detroit. He is married and has two daughters.

This book was brought to life by a great group of people:

Shannon Gilligan, Publisher
Gordon Troy, General Counsel
Jason Gellar, Sales Director
Melissa Bounty, Senior Editor
Stacey Boyd, Designer

Thanks to everyone involved!